Seafood

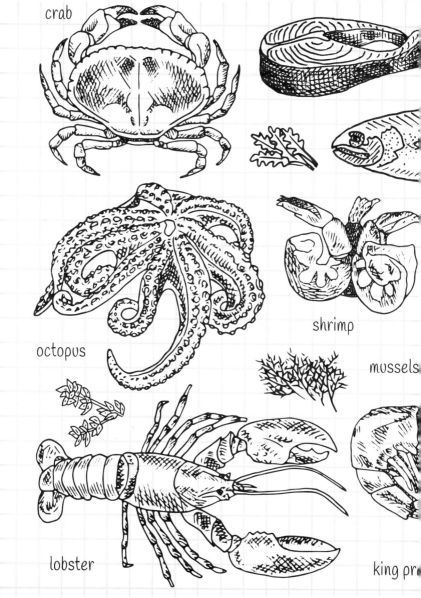

crab

octopus

shrimp

mussels

lobster

king pr

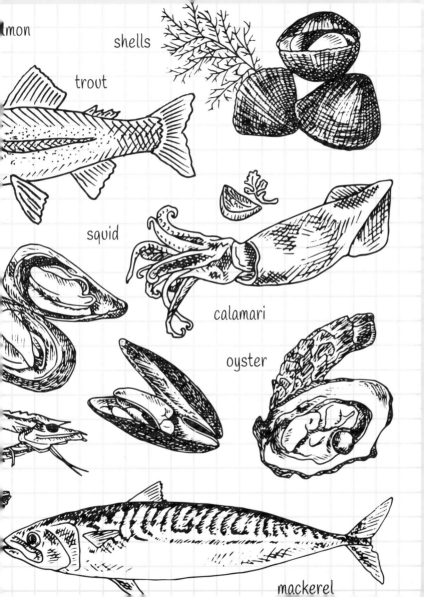

lmon

shells

trout

squid

calamari

oyster

mackerel

Introduction

Seafood is easy to prepare and endows a wide range of health benefits on those who eat it.

The world's oceans and inland waterways boast thousands of seafood species, and more than 300 of those are harvested commercially and caught by recreational fishers.

We are also increasingly conscious of the importance of sustainable fishing and the protection of endangered species.

Seafood is an integral part of our lifestyle.

Whether we are enjoying a sizzling summer's day, or in the middle of a snow storm in winter, we can choose a seafood dish to compliment the occasion.

This book offers a breakdown many of the perceived barriers people have about cooking with seafood.

The recipes are simple and easy to read and show that any type of seafood can be prepared easily for cooking.

Because these recipes incorporate seafood they are not only wonderfully tasty but also very healthy.

Seafood is an important element in a well-balanced diet. Seafood is particularly good for those on low-fat diets.

Research shows that eating fish two or three times a week is a sure recipe for a healthy lifestyle.The small amount of fat in fish is rich in omega-3 fatty acids, making fish a great heart food, as it helps to keep your arteries healthy.

Recent studies show that eating seafood can even help those with rheumatoid arthritis, and that it reduces the risk of asthma in children.

Seafood is good news for slimmers. All seafood is low in kilojoules, with fewer kilojoules than even the leanest meat or chicken, and of course you will not have to trim any fat. Just grill, broil, barbecue, bake, steam or poach seafood to keep a low kilojoule count.

Seafood is an excellent source of top-quality protein and minerals, including iodine, zinc, potassium and phosphorus. It is also rich in vitamins, especially the B group.

Buying and Storing Fish

When buying fish, make sure it is fresh, and if you plan to freeze it, don't buy fish that has already been frozen. There are a few things to look for to tell if fish is fresh:

- It should not have a strong odour. Instead it should have a pleasant and mild 'sea' smell.

- The flesh should be firm with a smooth, slippery skin and no yellow discolouration.

- Whole fish should have bright eyes and red gills

Oysters Kilpatrick

Serves 4-6

12 – 24 oysters in the half shell
1 teaspoon Worcestershire sauce
1 cup cream
salt and freshly ground black pepper
250g (9 oz) bacon strips, finely chopped
fine breadcrumbs

- Remove oysters from shells and put aside.

- Put shells on a baking sheet and heat in a moderate oven. Mix Worcestershire sauce and cream.

- When shells are hot, return oysters to shells. Use tongs to handle the shells, as they get very hot.

- Add a little of the cream mixture to each shell and sprinkle with salt and pepper.

- Top each oyster with chopped bacon and fine breadcrumbs. Place under a hot grill and grill until bacon is crisp but not burnt and oysters are warmed through.

Note: Oysters Kilpatrick are very tasty served with a bowl of hot puréed spinach and thin slices of buttered brown or rye bread.

Tempura Oysters

Serves 6-8

24 oysters
sunflower oil for deep frying

DIPPING SAUCE

¾ cup of soy sauce
⅓ cup water
4 tablespoon of brown sugar
1 tablespoon of lime juice
1 tablespoon of cornflour

- Heat soy sauce and water in a sauce pot over medium heat.

- Once hot, add the sugar and lime juice and turn heat to low.

- Mix the cornflour and a tablespoon of water together until combined in a small cup, then add it to the soy sauce mixture. Stir till the sauce thickens.

- Set aside to to cool and then pour into dipping saucers to serve.

TEMPURA BATTER

½ cup cornstarch (cornflour)
½ cup plain (all-purpose) flour
small pinch of salt

4 teaspoons toasted sesame seeds
¾ cup ice cold soda water
1 lime, cut into wedges

- Open all the oysters and pour off any liquid.

- Carefully cut the meat out of the deeper shells and retain the shells for serving.

- To make the dipping sauce, combine the soy sauce and lime juice with ⅓ cup water and pour into 4 dipping saucers.

- Heat the sunflower oil to 190°C (375°F).

- Make the batter by sifting the cornstarch, flour and salt into a mixing bowl. Stir in the sesame seeds then stir in the ice cold soda water until just mixed. Add a little more water if it seems too thick. The batter should be very thin and almost transparent.

- Dip the oysters one at a time into the batter.

- Drop into the hot oil and fry for a minute until crisp and golden. Lift out and drain on absorbent paper.

- Return the oysters to their shells and arrange on plates.

- Serve with lime wedges and the dipping sauce.

Grilled Oysters with Champagne

Serves 4

12 fresh oysters in their shells, pre-shucked
½ cup fish stock
¼ cup Champagne
30g (1 oz) butter
2 tablespoons thickened cream
freshly ground black pepper
50g (1¾ oz) baby spinach

- Place the oyster shells in a flameproof dish lined with crumpled foil so that the shells sit level.

- Bring the fish stock to a simmer and poach the oysters for 30–60 seconds, until just firm. Remove oysters from the pan, add the Champagne and boil for 2 minutes to reduce.

- Remove from the heat and whisk in the butter, then the cream. Season with pepper. Preheat the grill to high. Cook the spinach in a saucepan of water for 2–3 minutes until wilted.

- Squeeze out the excess liquid and divide between the shells. Top with an oyster and spoon over a little sauce. Cook close to the grill for 1 minute or until heated through.

Oysters Greta Garbo

Serves 4

12 oysters in shells
juice of ½ lime or lemon
6 slices smoked salmon, cut into fine strips
1 cup sour cream
2 tablespoons fresh chives,
chopped, for garnish
red caviar for garnish
crushed ice for serving

- Sprinkle the oysters with lime or lemon juice and top with smoked salmon.

- Put a dollop of the sour cream onto each oyster.

- Garnish with chives and red caviar.

- Serve on a bed of ice with a slice of lime.

Oysters with Parmesan Butter

Serves 4- 6

12 large oysters, shucked
100g (3½ oz) parmesan butter
rock salt, to taste
lemon wedges, to serve
Tabasco sauce, to serve

- Place 1 teaspoon of butter onto each oyster.

- Place the oysters on a hot barbecue grill and close the lid for 2-3 minutes until the butter melts.

- Leave to cool slightly as the shells will be hot.

- Place on a serving platter scattered with rock salt to seat the oyster (so you don't lose the butter).

- Serve with a few wedges of lemon and hot sauce such as Tabasco

Parmesan, Garlic and Parsley Butter

100g (3½ oz) softened butter
3 tablespoons finely grated parmesan cheese
1 garlic clove, crushed
2 tablespoons chopped flat-leaf parsley
salt and pepper, to taste

- Mix the ingredients in a bowl until smooth.

- Place the mixture onto a piece of plastic wrap and roll into a tube shape, twisting the ends and tie.

- Place in the freezer until firm, then cut into slices just before use.

San Francisco Seafood Chowder

Serves 8

8 smallish round loaves of bread
55g (2 oz) butter
2 leeks, rinsed and finely sliced
2 onions, finely chopped
4 cloves garlic, minced
2 carrots, peeled and chopped
1 parsnip, peeled and chopped
2 stalks celery, finely sliced
1 tablespoon fresh thyme leaves
½ cup plain flour
8 cups fish stock
1kg (2lbs) mixed seafood (including prawns/shrimp, mussels, clams, calamari/squid, white fish
200ml (7fl oz) thickened cream
1 cup fresh parsley, chopped
salt and pepper, to taste
juice of 1 large lemon
½ bunch chives, chopped, for garnish

- Preheat the oven to 200°C/400°F.

- First, prepare bread for bowls. Using a sharp knife, cut a large hole in the top of the bread loaf, then remove this crusty top and set aside.

- Carefully remove all the soft bread from the inside of the loaf (leaving the surrounding crust intact).

- Place the loaves in the preheated oven and bake for 15 minutes (until the loaves are crisp and dry). Set aside.

- Melt the butter in a large saucepan and add the leeks, onions, garlic, carrots, parsnip, celery and thyme leaves. Sauté for 10 minutes until the vegetables are soft and golden.

- Remove the pan from the heat and sprinkle flour over the vegetables, stirring constantly to mix flour with the butter. Return the pan to the heat and continue stirring until the mixture begins to turn golden (about 2 minutes). This gives the flour a 'cooked' taste.

- Add the fish stock stirring constantly to dissolve the roux mixture into the liquid, then simmer the soup for 20 minutes.

- Meanwhile, prepare the seafood by cutting the fish and shellfish into bite-sized pieces.

Add all the seafood, cream, parsley and salt and pepper, and cook for a further 5 minutes. (Do not allow the soup to boil rapidly because it may curdle.)

Once the seafood has cooked, stir the lemon juice through the fish and ladle the soup into the bread bowls.

Garnish with chives and serve.

Clam Chowder

Serves 4

255g (9 oz) butter
6 rashes of bacon, finely chopped
3 onions, finely chopped
1½ cups finely chopped celery
1 cup plain flour
4 cups milk
3 cups fish stock
500g (1lb) potatoes, finely diced
1kg (2lb) clam meat
salt and pepper
cream (optional), to serve
10 tablespoons chopped fresh parsley

- Heat the butter in a saucepan and cook the bacon, onion and celery until tender.

- Add the flour and cook for 2 minutes.

- Add milk, fish stock and potatoes, cover and simmer for 10 minutes.

- Add the clam meat and cook again for 10 minutes. Season to taste.

- Serve in a deep plate with cream and parsley.

Mussel Soup

Serves 2

300ml (10fl oz) water
1 small carrot, finely diced
55g (2 oz) cauliflower, divided into florets
½ red capsicum/pepper, finely diced
½ onion, finely diced
1 pinch saffron
10 coriander/cilantro seeds, cracked
45ml (1½ fl oz) sherry vinegar
55g (2 oz) butter
2 tablespoons plain flour
1kg (2 lbs) mussels, cooked mariniéres style,
reserving cooking broth.
2 tablespoons double cream
1 tablespoon parsley, finely chopped

- Place the water, carrot, cauliflower, capsicum, onion, saffron and coriander seeds in a large pot over high heat.

- Bring to the boil and add the vinegar.

- Remove from the heat and allow to cool down.

- When cold, strain the vegetables from the cooking liquid. In a cooking pot over medium heat, melt the butter then add the flour. Stir with a wooden spoon and cook gently for 2 minutes.

- Add the broth slowly with a whisk and cook until slightly thickened and smooth in consistency.

- Add the reserved vegetables, mussels and cream and bring to boil.

- Add salt and pepper to taste. Garnish with parsley just before serving.

Clam Bisque

Serves 4

500g (1 lb) white fish fillets
3 cups milk
salt and pepper, to taste
⅛ teaspoon nutmeg
1 bay leaf
250g (8 oz) jar mussels
2 tablespoons butter
1 medium-sized onion, finely chopped
2 stalks celery, finely cubed
3 tablespoons plain flour
1 tablespoon lemon juice
1 tablespoon finely chopped parsley or chives
1-2 tablespoons dry sherry
¼ cup cream

- Cut the fish fillets into 2cm (¾ in) squares.

- Place in a saucepan with the milk, salt, pepper, nutmeg and bay leaf. Bring gently to the boil, then simmer slowly for 10 minutes. Stand covered for 10 minutes to infuse the flavours.

- Strain the milk from the fish and reserve.

- Keep the fish warm.

- Drain the liquid from the mussels and rinse in cold water. Cut the mussels into 2 or 3 pieces.

- Melt the butter in a large saucepan, add the onion and celery and cook gently for 10 minutes without browning. When soft, stir in the flour and cook for 1 minute while stirring.

- Remove the saucepan from the heat and gradually stir in the reserved milk, stirring well after each addition until free from lumps.

- Return to the heat and stir until the mixture boils and thickens.

- Add the lemon juice, chopped mussels, chopped parsley, sherry and cooked fish. Simmer slowly for 10 minutes.

- Stir in the cream and simmer for 5 minutes more.

- Serve in individual bowls, with croutons if desired.

Lobster Bisque

Serves 4

1 small lobster, cooked
1 large carrot, peeled and diced
1 small onion, finely chopped
125g (4½ oz) butter
¾ cup dry white wine
bouquet garni
6½ cups fish or chicken stock
¾ cup rice
salt, pepper and ground cayenne
½ cup cream
2 tablespoons brandy
chopped parsley

- Split the lobster in half lengthwise, and remove the flesh from the shell. Set aside.

- Wrap the shell in a clean tea towel, crush the shell with a hammer and set aside.

- Sauté the carrot and onion in half the butter until softened (about 5 minutes). Add the crushed shell, sauté a further minute or so then add the wine. Boil rapidly until reduced by half. Add the bouquet garni, stock and rice.

- After about 20 minutes, when the rice is tender, remove the large pieces of shell and the bouquet garni.

- Purée small batches in a food processor with the remainder of the batter, doing so in small batches.

- Pour through a strainer. Rinse out the food processor to remove every trace of shell and purée the strained liquid again, this time with the lobster flesh, saving a few pieces for the garnish.

- Reheat gently.

- Taste, add salt, pepper and cayenne to taste then stir in the cream, brandy and reserved lobster pieces, cut into thin slices.

- Serve very hot garnished with parsley.

Grilled Sardines

Serves 3-4

12 sardines, cleaned
¼ cup extra virgin olive oil
sea salt
1 lemon, cut into wedges

- Place sardines in a large shallow ceramic dish.

- Drizzle with olive oil and sprinkle over salt, cover with cling wrap and refrigerate for 1-2 hours.

- Preheat a grill or barbecue.

- Cook sardines for 3-4 minutes each side or until golden and cooked.

Tuna Ceviche

Serves 4

500g (17½ oz) tuna steaks, diced
½ small red onion, thinly sliced
2 tablespoons extra virgin olive oil
Juice of one large lime
1 teaspoon Dijon mustard
¼ teaspoon sugar
2 cloves garlic, crushed
1 long red chilli, deseeded and finely chopped
salt and freshly ground black pepper
1 tablespoon roughly chopped roasted peanuts
2 spring onions, sliced
¼ cup coriander (cilantro), freshly chopped

- Place fish and red onion in a ceramic dish.

- Whisk together olive oil, lime juice, Dijon mustard, sugar, garlic and chilli in a jug.

- Pour over fish and toss well. Season with salt and pepper. Cover with cling wrap and refrigerate for 1 hour.

- Sprinkle with peanuts, spring onions and coriander and serve with lime wedges.

Fish Cakes

Serves 2

4 slices bread, crusts removed
700g (1lb 8 oz) floury potatoes, halved or quartered
depending on size
3 tablespoons mayonnaise
400g (14 oz) canned tuna in oil, drained and flaked
or smoked salmon fresh or from a can
¼ cup parsley, chopped
2 spring onions, finely chopped
finely grated zest of 1 small lemon
3 tablespoons plain flour
1 medium egg, beaten
vegetable oil for frying

- Preheat the oven to 160°C (325°F).

- Place the bread on a baking sheet and cook at
  the bottom of the oven for 20–30 minutes until
  crisp.

- Cool, break into pieces and crush with a rolling
  pin.

- Meanwhile, cook the potatoes in a large saucepan of boiling salted water for 15 minutes or until tender. Drain, transfer to a bowl and mash with the mayonnaise.

- Leave to cool for 30 minutes.

- Mash the tuna, parsley, spring onions and lemon zest into the potatoes. Flour your hands, then shape the mixture into 8 flat cakes. Dust with flour and dip into the egg, then into the breadcrumbs.

- Heat 5mm (⅛ in) of oil in a large heavy-based frying pan and cook the fish cakes for 3–4 minutes on each side until crisp and golden (you may have to cook them in batches).

- Drain on absorbent paper, then serve with the lemon wedges.

Note:

These chunky fish cakes are packed with flavour and it only takes a few vegetables or a salad to make a complete meal.

Canned salmon works just as well as the tuna.

Mixed Shellfish and Potato Salad

Serves 4

680g (1½ lb) waxy potatoes, unpeeled
4 small cooked beetroot, diced
1 head fennel, finely sliced, plus feathery top, chopped
1kg (2 lb) mussels
510g (18 oz) clams
285ml (10fl oz) dry white wine or apple cider
1 eschallot/French shallot finely chopped
4 spring onions/scallions, finely sliced
3 tablespoons chopped fresh parsley

DRESSING

5 tablespoons olive oil
1 tablespoons cider vinegar
1 teaspoon English mustard
salt and pepper

- To make the dressing, whisk together the oil, vinegar, mustard and seasoning.

- Boil the potatoes in salted water for 15 minutes or until tender, then drain. Cool for 30 minutes, then peel and slice.

◄ Place in a bowl and toss with half the dressing. Toss the beetroot and fennel with the rest of the dressing.

◄ Scrub the mussels and clams under cold running water, pulling away any beards from the mussels. Discard any shellfish that are open or damaged. Place the wine or cider and shallot in a large saucepan and bring to the boil. Simmer for 2 minutes, then add the shellfish.

◄ Cover and cook briskly for 3–5 minutes, shaking the pan often, or until the shellfish have opened. Discard any that remain closed. Reserve the pan juices, set aside a few mussels in their shells and shell the rest.

◄ Boil the pan juices for 5 minutes or until reduced to 1–2 tablespoons. Strain over the potatoes. Add the shellfish, spring onions and parsley, then toss.

◄ Serve with the beetroot and fennel salad and garnish with the fennel tops and mussels in their shells.

Lobster Salad

Serves 4

2 medium-sized lobsters, cooked
4 lettuce cups
150 ml (5 fl oz) mayonnaise
2 lemons, juiced
2 tomatoes, sliced
½ avocado, sliced
parsley, finely chopped

- Crack the lobster claws with a light weight. If you have special lobster picks, leave the meat in the cracked shells, otherwise carefully take out the meat with a fine skewer. If leaving the meat in the claws, arrange these beside the body of the lobster.

- Remove meat from the shell, dice and place back in the shell.

- If removing the meat from the claws, blend it with the body meat.

- Arrange lobster on lettuce, and top with some mayonnaise.

- Mix together the lemon juice, tomatoes, avocado and parsley and serve on the side.

Calamari Salad With Basil Dressing

Serves 4

300g (10 oz) calamari tubes, washed
and sliced into 1cm (½ in) rings
250ml (8fl oz) water
80ml (2⅔fl oz) lemon juice
80ml (2⅔fl oz) grapeseed oil
150g (5 oz) snow peas, trimmed
100g (3½ oz) button mushrooms
1 punnet cherry tomatoes
1 green capsicum (bell pepper), seeds and pith
removed and cut into strips
2 tablespoons chives, chopped

BASIL DRESSING

60ml (2fl oz) French dressing
½ cup chopped fresh basil

- Cook calamari in simmering water for 2 minutes or until cooked. Drain.

- Combine lemon juice and grapeseed oil. Pour mixture into a bowl and add calamari. Toss calamari until coated.

- Cover bowl with cling wrap and refrigerate overnight.

- Place snow peas, mushrooms, tomatoes, capsicum and chives into a salad bowl.

- Drain calamari, reserving marinade. Add calamari to salad and chill for 30 minutes, covered. In a bowl or jar, combine dressing ingredients and reserved marinade.

- Chill for 30 minutes.

- Just before serving, drizzle dressing over salad and toss lightly.

Crab Salad

Serves 4

400g (14 oz) crabmeat, fresh or canned
4 crisp celery sticks, finely chopped
125ml (4fl oz) French dressing
salt and freshly ground black pepper, to taste
4 small butter lettuces, shredded
4 sprigs chives, to garnish

- In a mixing bowl, combine crabmeat and celery. Moisten with French dressing and salt and pepper and mix well.

- Line a salad bowl with the shredded lettuce.

- Pile the crab on top.

- Add some more dressing, scatter with chives just before serving.

Garlic Shrimp Salad

Serves 4

1 tablespoon extra-virgin olive oil
4 cloves garlic, crushed
½ teaspoon red pepper flakes
24 large shrimp, peeled and deveined
1 medium tomato, sliced
1 head of cos (romaine) lettuce
1 English cucumber, sliced into ribbons
salt and freshly ground black pepper
juice of 1 lime
juice of 1 lemon

- Heat a large heavy-based skillet, add the oil, garlic, red pepper flakes and shrimp. Cook, stirring constantly, until the shrimp are cooked, about 3 minutes.

- Divide the tomato slices between 4 serving plates, top with lettuces leaves and cucumber ribbons.

- Add the shrimp and pour over the pan juices.

- Season with salt and pepper, then squeeze the lemon and lime juices over and serve.

Grilled Shrimp

Serves 2- 4

1kg (2lb) green shrimp, peeled and deveined

MARINADE

250ml (8fl oz) olive oil
60ml (2fl oz) lemon juice
75g (2½ oz) onion, finely chopped
2 cloves garlic, crushed
parsley, finely chopped

- To make marinade, place all marinade ingredients in a large bowl and mix well. Add shrimp to the bowl and combine.

- Cover bowl and let stand for several hours in the refrigerator. Drain shrimp.

- Place shrimp in a heavy-based frying pan or skillet and cook over medium coals for 10–15 minutes, or until cooked.

- Stir frequently and add a little marinade while cooking.

- Serve immediately.

Clams with White Wine and Garlic

Serves 4

680g (1½ lb) medium to small clams
salt and pepper
45ml (1½ fl oz) olive oil
1 small onion, peeled and finely chopped
3 cloves garlic, peeled and minced
1 tablespoon plain flour
100ml (3½ fl oz) dry white wine
pinch of paprika
1 bay leaf
salt and pepper to taste

- Wash the clams well, leave them in cold water and add a little salt for about an hour.

- Heat oil in a frying pan. Add the onion and garlic and sauté until golden brown. Add clams and cook over medium heat until the shells open. Add the flour and stir in well. Pour in the wine, add the paprika, bay leaf and some salt and pepper to taste.

- Continue cooking for a further 5 minutes.

- Remove the bay leaf and serve the clams in the sauce.

Baked Mussels

Serves 4

28 medium mussels
2 shallots/spring onions, finely chopped
1 sprig thyme
2 sprigs parsley
1 bay leaf
½ teaspoon salt
½ cup white wine
115g (4 oz) butter or margarine, softened
1 tablespoon parsley, chopped
2 cloves garlic, crushed
1 tablespoon chives

- Scrape the beard, and wash the mussels thoroughly.

- In a large saucepan with the shallots, thyme, parsley and bay leaf. Add salt over and then add the wine. Steam for 5 minutes or until the shells have opened. Open the mussels and discard the lids.

- Divide the mussels in the remaining half shells into 4 ovenproof dishes. Make a herb butter by combining the butter, parsley, garlic and chives and place a generous portion on each mussel.

- Bake at 190°C (370°F) for approximately 3 minutes or until the butter has melted and serve.

Mussels with Tomatoes and Wine

Serves 4

1kg (2 lb) fresh mussels, scrubbed and beards
removed
1 shallot (spring onion, chopped
1 cup dry white wine
chopped fresh chives

TOMATO AND SMOKED SALMON SAUCE

2 teaspoons olive oil
2 cloves garlic, crushed
2 shallots, chopped
2-3 slices smoked salmon, sliced into thin strips
1 red bell pepper (capsicum), sliced
1 tablespoon no-added-salt tomato paste
400g (14 oz) canned no added-salt diced tomatoes
2 tablespoons chopped fresh parsley

- For the sauce, heat the oil in a non-stick frying
  pan over a medium heat. Add the garlic and
  shallots.

- Cook, stirring, for 1-2 minutes. Add the salmon
  and red bell pepper (capsicum).

- Cook, stirring, for 3 minutes. Stir in the tomato paste.

- Cook for 3–4 minutes or until it becomes deep red and develops a rich aroma. Add the tomatoes. Cook, stirring, for 5 minutes or until the mixture starts to thicken. Stir in the parsley. Keep warm.

- Meanwhile, place the mussels, shallots and wine in a large saucepan over a high heat. Cover. Bring to the boil then reduce the heat. Cook for 5 minutes or until the mussels open.

- Discard any mussels that do not open after 5 minutes of cooking.

- Add the sauce to the mussels. Toss to combine.

- To serve, divide the mixture among deep bowls. Scatter with chives.

- Accompany with crusty bread and a glass of red wine.

Bacon-wrapped Scallops with spicy mayo

Serves 2-4

12 streaky bacon strips
12 large sea scallops
½ teaspoon garlic powder
salt and pepper, to taste
lemon wedges, to serve

SPICY MAYO

60g (2.1 oz) mayonnaise
2 tablespoons tomato sauce
1 tablespoon hot sauce
2 lemons (juiced)

- Cook the bacon on a medium heat till cooked.

- Once cooled, wrap each scallop with a slice of bacon and secure it with a toothpick. Squeeze over the lemon juice and garlic powder, then season with salt and pepper and cook on medium heat on BBQ flat plate or in an oiled fray pan. until bacon is crispy and scallops are firm and cooked.

- Meanwhile, make the spicy seafood sauce. Mix together the mayonnaise, tomato sauce, hot sauce and lemon juice in a bowl.

- Refrigerate until needed. Serve the scallops while still warm with lemon wedges and spicy mayo.

Spaghetti Marinara

Serves 4

510g (18 oz) spaghetti
2 teaspoons vegetable oil - 2 teaspoons butter
2 onions, chopped
2 x 400g (14 oz) canned tomatoes, mashed
2 tablespoons chopped fresh basil or 1 tsp of dried
¼ cup/60ml (2fl oz) dry white wine
12 mussels, scrubbed and beards removed
12 scallops - 12 raw prawns/shrimp, shelled and
deveined - 115g (4 oz) calamari/squid rings

- Cook the pasta in boiling water in a large saucepan following the packet directions. Drain, set aside.

- Heat the oil and butter in a frying pan over medium heat. Add the onions and cook, stirring, until the onions are golden.

- Stir in the tomatoes, basil and wine and simmer for 8 minutes. Add the mussels, scallops and prawns and cook for 2 minutes longer. Add the calamari and cook for 1 minute or until the shellfish is cooked.

- Spoon the seafood mixture over hot pasta and serve immediately.

Mussels Mariniéres

Serves 4

1kg (2lb) mussels, cleaned
1 small onion, sliced
1 stalk celery, sliced
1 clove garlic, chopped
55ml (2fl oz) water or white wine
pepper
1 tablespoon butter
1 tablespoon parsley, chopped

- Place the mussels, onion, celery, garlic and water (or white wine) in a large saucepan.

- Cook over medium heat until the mussels have opened, about 5 minutes. Stir frequently to ensure the mussels cook evenly.

- Add pepper to taste. Stir in the butter and parsley just before serving.

Mussel Risotto

Serves 4

200ml (7fl oz) olive oil
1 onion, finely chopped
2 cloves garlic, finely chopped
1 red capsicum/pepper, diced
285g (10 oz) arborio rice
2¼ cups dry white wine
1kg (2lb) mussels, cleaned
1 tablespoon chopped fresh aromatic herbs
2 tablespoons grated Parmesan cheese
sliced chives, to serve

- Place the oil in a pot over medium heat.

- Add the onion, garlic and capsicum and cook for 2 minutes.

- Add rice and half the wine. Stir with a wooden spatula and cook until the rice is almost dry.

- Add mussels and the other half of the wine.

- Add the herbs and cook until the rice and mussels are cooked. Replace the lid and stir frequently to avoid the rice sticking to the pot.

- Serve sprinkled with grated Parmesan and sliced chives.

Salt and Pepper Squid

Serves 4

750g (1½ lb) squid tubes (squid hoods)
260g (9 oz) plain (all-purpose) flour
sea salt and pepper
2-3 eggs
60 ml (2fl oz) milk
120g (4 oz) panko breadcrumbs
oil, for deep-frying
lemon wedges, to serve

- Cut squid tubes into 5 mm (¼ inch) rings. Place the rings on absorbent paper and dry well.

- Sift plain flour into a bowl and season with salt and pepper. Whisk eggs and milk together in a shallow bowl.

- Toss the squid rings into the flour, one at a time, then dip into the egg mixture, shaking off any extra liquid. Toss rings in panko breadcrumbs to coat. Heat oil to medium-high heat (it may spit and splatter, so be careful).

- Cook the rings in the hot oil until golden brown (3 minutes maximum). Drain well and serve hot with lemon wedges.

Seafood Paella

Serves 6-8

1 tablespoon olive oil
2 onions, chopped
2 cloves garlic, crushed
1 tablespoon fresh thyme leaves
2 teaspoons finely grated lemon rind
4 ripe tomatoes, chopped
2½ cups short-grain white rice
pinch saffron threads soaked in 2 cups water
5 cups chicken or fish stock
285g (10 oz) fresh or frozen peas
2 red capsicums/peppers, chopped
1kg (2lb) mussels, scrubbed and beards removed
510g (18 oz) firm white fish fillets, chopped
285g (10 oz) peeled uncooked prawns/shrimp
225g (8 oz) scallops
3 calamari/squid tubes, sliced
1 tablespoon chopped fresh parsley

Preheat the barbecue to a medium heat.

Place a large paella or frying pan on the barbecue, add the oil and heat. Add the onions, garlic, thyme leaves and lemon rind and cook for 3 minutes or until the onion is soft.

Add the tomatoes and cook, stirring, for 4 minutes. Add the rice and cook, stirring, for 4 minutes longer or until the rice is translucent.

Stir in the saffron mixture and stock and bring to a simmer. Simmer, stirring occasionally, for 30 minutes or until the rice has absorbed almost all of the liquid.

Stir in the peas, capsicums and mussels and cook for 2 minutes.

Add the fish, prawns and scallops and cook, stirring, for 2-3 minutes.

Stir in calamari and parsley and cook, stirring, for 1-2 minutes longer or until the seafood is cooked.

Honey and Chilli Prawns/Shrimp

Serves 4

¼ cup red wine
½ cup honey
¼ teaspoon ground chilli
1 teaspoon mustard powder
500g (1lb) green king prawns/shrimp
bamboo skewers (soaked in water for 30 minutes)

- Mix all ingredients except prawns together to make marinade.

- Shell the prawns, leaving on the tails, and devein.

- Place in a glass dish and add enough marinade to coat well. Cover and marinate in refrigerator for 1 hour.

- Thread the prawns onto skewers, either through the side or through the length.

- Heat the barbecue to medium-high. Place a sheet of foil over the grill bars and place the prawns on the paper. Cook for 4–5 minutes each side: they will turn pink when cooked. Brush with marinade while cooking.

- Transfer to a platter. If liked, remove prawns from skewers and serve immediately with lemon and parsley.

Char-Grilled Baby Octopus Salad

Serves 4

375g (13 oz) baby octopus, cleaned
1 teaspoon sesame oil
1 tablespoon lime juice
¼ cup sweet chilli sauce
1 tablespoon fish sauce
60g (2 oz) rice noodle vermicelli
125g (4 oz) mixed salad leaves
1 cup bean sprouts
1 Lebanese cucumber, halved
200g (7 oz) cherry tomatoes, halved
½ cup fresh coriander (cilantro) sprigs
2 limes, cut into wedges

- Rinse the cleaned octopus and pat dry with absorbent paper.

- Put the sesame oil, lime juice, sweet chilli sauce and fish sauce in a jug and whisk to combine.

- Pour over the octopus and coat with the marinade. Cover with cling wrap and marinate for 4 hours or overnight. Drain and reserve the marinade.

- Put the vermicelli in a bowl, cover with boiling water and allow to stand for 10 minutes or until soft. Drain well.

- Divide the mixed salad leaves among 4 plates, top with the bean sprouts, rice vermicelli, cucumber and tomatoes.

- Cook the octopus on a preheated chargrill or barbecue until tender and well coloured. Put the marinade in a small pot and bring to the boil.

- Serve the octopus on top of the salad, drizzle with the hot marinade and garnish with coriander and lime wedges.

Spicy Barbecued baby Octopus

Serves 4-6

1kg (35 oz) baby octopus
400ml (13.5fl oz) red wine
100ml (3.4fl oz) balsamic vinegar
1 garlic clove, crushed
50ml (1.7fl oz) soy sauce
50ml (1.7fl oz) hot sauce
50ml (1.7fl oz) barbecue sauce
50ml (1.7fl oz) tomato sauce
salt and pepper, to taste
20g (0.7 oz) chopped fresh coriander
1 lemon, cut into wedges

- Place the octopus, red wine and balsamic vinegar in a saucepan and bring to the boil over medium heat. Reduce to a simmer for 15 minutes.

- Drain the octopus, then place in a large bowl. Combine the garlic, soy sauce, hot sauce, tomato sauce and barbecue sauce. Add to the octopus and mix to ensure the octopus is well coated.

- Cook the octopus on a hot barbecue grill side, while basting with the sauce, for about 5 minutes or until charred. Serve with lemon and garnish with coriander.

Angels on Horseback

Serves 4-6

12 large oysters, freshly shucked or from a bottle
6 streaky bacon strips
lemon wedges, to serve

- Cut each slice of bacon in half and wrap the oysters in bacon.

- Overlap the ends, securing with a toothpick or short skewer.

- On hot grill, cook until the bacon is crisp (depending on the thickness of your bacon).

- Serve while warm with a wedge of lemon.

Butterflied Shrimp/Prawns with Garlic, Chilli & Parsley

Serves 4

1kg (2lb) (approx 20) green prawns/ shrimp, shelled,
deveined, tails intact
2 tablespoons olive oil
1 tablespoon lemon juice
2 cloves garlic, crushed
2 red chillies, de-seeded and finely chopped
2 tablespoons parsley, chopped
oil (for frying)
½ cup plain/all-purpose flour (for coating prawns)
lemon wedges and extra parsley (to garnish)

- Cut prawns down the back and remove vein.

- Combine oil, lemon juice, garlic, chilli and parsley in a bowl. Add prawns, mix well, and leave to marinate for 2-3 hours.

- Heat oil in a large pan, coat prawns with flour, and cook quickly in oil for 2-3 minutes. Drain on absorbent paper towels.

- Serve with lemon wedges and parsley.

Jambalaya

Serves 4

3 strips bacon, cut into pieces
1 large onion, finely chopped
1 green capsicum/bell pepper, diced
1 stalk celery, chopped
3 cloves garlic, crushed
1 cup long-grain rice
1½–3 cups boiling chicken stock
398ml (14fl oz) can tomatoes, drained and mashed
2 teaspoons Cajun spice mix
1 teaspoon dried thyme
500g (1lb) uncooked medium prawns/shrimp, shelled and deveined
155g (5½ oz) smoked ham in one piece, cut into 1cm (½ in) cubes
3 shallots/spring onions, finely chopped

- Cook bacon in a frying pan over a medium heat for 5 minutes or until crisp.

- Remove bacon from pan and drain on paper towels.

- Add onion to pan and cook, stirring, for 5 minutes or until onion is soft, but not brown.

- Add capsicum, celery and garlic and cook for 3 minutes.

- Add rice and cook, stirring frequently, for 5 minutes or until rice becomes translucent.

- Stir in stock, tomatoes, spice mix and thyme and bring to the boil.

- Cover, reduce heat to low and cook for 15 minutes. Stir in prawns, bacon and ham, cover and cook for 10 minutes longer or until rice is tender and liquid absorbed.

- Sprinkle with shallots and serve immediately.

Fish and Chips with Tartare Sauce

Serves 4

90g (3 oz) plain (all-purpose) flour
½ teaspoon salt
1 tablespoon vegetable oil
4 large potatoes, cut into chunkyb chips
vegetable oil for deep-frying
1 large egg white
4 pieces white fish fillets, about
170g (6 oz) each

TARTARE SAUCE

¾ cup mayonnaise
1 tablespoon capers, drained and chopped
1 gherkin, chopped
¼ cup parsley, chopped
1 French shallot, finely chopped

- To make sauce, combine mayonnaise, capers, gherkin, parsley and shallot in a bowl. Cover and place in the refrigerator.

- Mix flour, salt and oil with ½ cup cold water to make a batter.

- Cover chips with cold water, then drain and dry on absorbent paper. Heat oil in a large heavy-based saucepan. Test that oil is ready by adding a potato chip—it should sizzle immediately.

- Cook chips in 3 or 4 batches for 5-7 minutes each, until golden and cooked. Drain on absorbent paper and keep warm.

- Whisk egg white until stiff and fold into the batter.

- Reduce the heat a little and drop a teaspoon of batter into the oil—it should bubble and firm up straight away.

- Dip pieces of fish into batter, coating well, then cook for 5-7 minutes, until crisp and golden, then drain on absorbent paper.

- Sprinkle with salt and serve with chips and tartare sauce.

Lobster Toasts

Serves 6

255g (9 oz) cream cheese
55g (2 oz) unsalted butter
55g (2 oz) cooked lobster meat
1 tablespoon olive oil
juice of ½ lemon
salt and pepper, to taste
extra olive oil, for serving
12 slices of French baguette, or Turkish bread, toasted
fresh parsley, chopped, for garnish

- Combine all the ingredients, except toast and parsley in a food processor and blend until creamy.

- Spread on the toast and heat through under a preheated hot grill before serving.

- Sprinkle with chopped parsley and ground black pepper, drizzle with some olive oil and serve.

Scampi with Basil Butter

Serves 2-4

8 uncooked scampi or yabbies, heads removed
Basil Butter
85g (3 oz) butter, melted
2 tablespoons chopped fresh basil
1 clove garlic, crushed
2 teaspoons honey

- Cut the scampi or yabbies in half, lengthwise.

- To make the basil butter, place the butter, basil, garlic and honey in a small bowl and whisk to combine.

- Brush the cut side of each scampi or yabbie half with basil butter and cook under a preheated hot grill for 2 minutes or until the shells turn red and are tender.

- Drizzle with any remaining basil butter and serve immediately.

Grilled Scampi with Herb Butter

Serves 4

10–12 scampi or yabbies
140g (5 oz) butter
few sprigs fresh herbs, chopped
2 tablespoons chopped parsley
2 cloves garlic, finely chopped
salt and freshly ground pepper
lemon wedges, to serve

- Split the scampi or yabbies lengthwise and arrange, cut side up, on a large shallow dish.

- Melt the butter and add the herbs and garlic. Drizzle butter mixture over the scampi and season with freshly ground pepper. (The scampi can be prepared ahead up to this stage.)

- Preheat the griller and arrange the scampi, cut side up, on the grilling pan.

- Cook for about 5 minutes until the flesh has turned white. Remove from the heat, season with salt and arrange on a large serving platter with wedges of lemon.

- To eat the scampi use a fork to pull out the tail meat.

- Place a bowl on the table for the discarded shells, and a few finger bowls, each with a squeeze of lemon.

Chilli Crab

Serves 4

2 medium or 1 large crab, or 6 blue swimmer crabs
3 tablespoons vegetable oil
1 tablespoon lemon juice
salt

SAUCE

2-3 red chillies, seeded and chopped
1 onion, peeled and chopped
2 cloves garlic, peeled and chopped
2 teaspoons grated fresh ginger
2 tablespoons vegetable oil
2 ripe tomatoes, skinned, seeded and chopped, or 2 teaspoons tomato paste
1 teaspoon sugar
1 tablespoon light soy sauce
3 tablespoons water

- Clean the crabs thoroughly, then cut each body into 2 or 4 pieces. Chop or crack the claws into 2 or 3 places if they are large.

- Heat the oil in a frying pan, add the crab pieces and fry for 5 minutes, stirring constantly. Add the lemon juice and salt to taste, remove from the heat and keep hot.

- To make the sauce, put the chillies, onion and garlic with ginger in a blender and work to a smooth paste.

- Heat the oil in a wok or deep frying pan. Add spice paste and fry for 1 minute, stirring constantly. Add the tomatoes, sugar and soy sauce and stir-fry for 2 minutes, then stir in the water. Add salt if necessary and simmer for a further 1 minute.

- Add the crab and stir to coat each piece in the sauce and cook the crab through, for only 1-2 minutes.

- Serve hot.

Lobster Lasagne

Serves 4-8

fresh lasagne sheets, prepared according to packet directions
255g (9 oz) chopped onion
30g (1 oz) butter
225g (8 oz) cream cheese, softened
1 egg, beaten
310g (11 oz) chopped dill pickles
2 teaspoons chopped basil
285ml (10fl oz) cans cream of mushroom soup
½ cup milk
85ml (3fl oz) white wine or chicken broth
85ml (3fl oz) seafood sauce
310g (11 oz) fresh or canned lobster meat, thawed and drained (several pieces of lobster meat can be set aside for a garnish, if desired)
285g (10 oz) scallops, thawed if frozen and cut in half
85g (3 oz) grated Parmesan cheese
255g (9 oz) mozzarella cheese

- Arrange 4 lasagne sheets to cover the bottom of an oiled 9 x 13 ins (23 x 33cm) baking dish. Sauté the onion in the butter just until tender. Stir in the cream cheese, egg, pickles and basil, mixing well. Spread half of this cheese mixture over the lasagne sheets.

- Preheat oven to 180°C (350°F.)

- Combine the soup, milk, wine, seafood sauce, lobster and scallops and fold over until well mixed. Spread half over the cheese mixture in the dish.

- Repeat layers with the remaining lasagne, cheese and seafood mixture. Sprinkle with Parmesan.

- Place in oven and bake uncovered for 40 minutes or until heated through. Sprinkle with mozzarella and bake for 2–3 minutes longer or until the cheese melts.

- Remove from the oven and let stand for 15 minutes before serving.

Lobster Mornay

Serves 2

medium lobster cooked and halved

MORNAY SAUCE

310ml (11fl oz) milk
1 bay leaf
1 small onion, chopped
5 black peppercorns
30g (1 oz) butter, plus 15ml (½ fl oz)
extra, melted
2 tablespoons plain flour
65ml (2¼fl oz) cream
65g (2¼ oz) cheese, grated
salt and cracked black peppercorns
65g (2¼ oz) fresh breadcrumbs
lemon wedges and salad, to serve

- Remove the lobster meat from the shells, reserve shells.

- Cut lobster meat into bite-sized pieces and set aside.

- In a saucepan, place the milk, bay leaf, onion and peppercorns. Heat slowly to boiling point. Remove from the heat, cover and stand for 10 minutes. Strain.

- In a pan, heat the butter, then remove from the heat. Stir in the flour and blend, gradually adding the strained milk. Return the pan to the heat, and stir constantly until the sauce boils and thickens.

- Simmer the sauce for 1 minute. Remove from the heat, add the cream, cheese, salt and pepper. Stir the sauce until the cheese melts, and add the lobster meat.

- Divide the lobster and sauce mixture between the shells. Melt extra butter in a small pan, add the breadcrumbs, and stir to combine.

- Pour the butter and crumbs over the lobster and brown under a preheated hot grill.

- Serve with lemon wedges and salad.

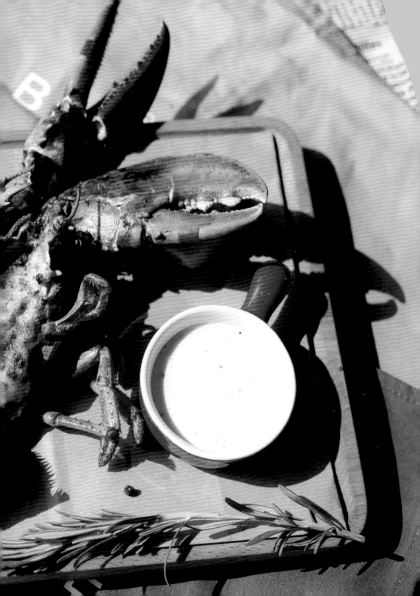

Fish Tacos

Serves 6

1 egg
100g (3½ oz) plain flour
½ teaspoon salt
1 teaspoon pepper
4 fillets of any firm flesh fish
3 tablespoons olive oil
1 tablespoon butter
six small soft tacos
sweet coleslaw

- Whisk the egg. Combine the flour, salt and pepper.

- Dip the fish fillets in the egg wash, then coat the fillets in the flour mix.

- Place the fish fillets on a medium-high heat barbecue flatplate with the oil and butter or in a fry pan on the stove. Cook for 3-4 minutes on each side, or until golden brown.

- Cut the fillets into long strips and place on the tacos with the sweet coleslaw.

- Garnish with coriander.

Fish Pie

Serves 4-6

1 kg (2¼ lb) potatoes, cut into even-sized pieces
salt and black pepper
55g (2 oz) butter
1 onion, chopped
2 sticks celery, sliced
2 tablespoons plain flour
1 cup fish stock
finely grated rind and juice of 1 large lemon
510g (18 oz) white fish, cut into cubes
170g (6 oz) cooked fish of your choice
2 talespoon chopped fresh parsley
4 tablespoon milk

- Cook the potatoes in boiling salted water for 15–20 minutes, until tender, then drain.

- Meanwhile, melt half of the butter in a large saucepan, then add the onion and celery and cook for 2–3 minutes, until softened.

- Add the flour and cook, stirring, for 1 minute, then slowly add the fish stock and cook, stirring, until thickened. Add the lemon rind and juice and season with pepper.

- Preheat the oven to 220°C (425°F).

- Remove the sauce from the heat, stir in the fish, and parsley, then transfer to an ovenproof dish.

- Mash the potatoes with the remaining butter and the milk. Season, then spread evenly over the fish with a fork.

- Cook in the oven for 30–40 minutes, until the sauce is bubbling and the topping is starting to brown.

Bouillabaisse

Serves 4

3 kg (6½ lb) fish heads and bones
4 tablespoons olive oil
3 cups dry white wine
4 carrots, peeled and sliced
2 leeks, washed and sliced
2 onions, peeled and sliced
3 sticks celery, sliced
6 tomatoes, chopped
1 teaspoon peppercorns
1 bunch of thyme, tied together
1 bunch parsley, tied together
1 bunch of dill, tied together
4 fresh bay leaves
12 cups of water
salt and pepper

SOUP

2 tablespoons olive oil
2 large leeks, washed and sliced
1 large fennel bulb, finely sliced
6 shallots, peeled and sliced
3 medium potatoes, peeled and diced
large pinch of saffron threads
2 x 400g (14 oz) cans Italianstyle tomatoes
2 kg (4½ lb) assorted fish fillets, diced
570g (20 oz) large prawns (shrimp), peeled
1kg (2¼ lb) mussels, scrubbed and rinsed
510g (18 oz) small calamari (squid), cleaned
1 bunch parsley, chopped
1 loaf sourdough bread
salt and pepper, to taste

FOR THE ROUILLE

2 large bell peppers (capsicums)
1 cup (125g) (4 oz) breadcrumbs
3 cloves garlic
1 teaspoon red wine vinegar
1 cup liquid from soup
2 small red chillies
olive oil
salt and pepper

- Rinse the fish heads and bones and set aside. Heat the olive oil in a deep saucepan and add the fish heads and bones.

- Cook the fish pieces over a high heat, stirring constantly, until the fish pieces begin to break down, scraping up anything that sticks to the bottom of the pan, (for about 20 minutes). Add the wine and simmer, stirring well. Add the prepared vegetables, herbs, bay leaves and water and simmer for 30 minutes, skimming any scum off the surfacebas it appears.

- After 30 minutes, strain the stock thoroughly, pressing on the solids to extract as much liquid as possible.

- Return to the heat for a further 20 minutes then add salt and pepper to taste. Set aside.

- To make the soup, heat the olive oil in a saucepan and add the sliced leeks, fennel, shallots, potatoes and saffron and cook over medium heat until all the vegetables are golden and soft, (about 20 minutes). Add the squashed canned tomatoes and reserved fish stock and bring the soup to the boil.

- Add salt and pepper to taste.

- Add the fish, prawns (shrimp) and mussels and simmer for 10 minutes. Add the calamari (squid) and parsley and stir gently. Remove the soup from the heat and cover. Allow to rest for 10 minutes.

- Meanwhile, brush the sliced sourdough bread with olive oil and grill until golden on both sides.

- Rub a clove of garlic over each golden slice. To serve, place a slice of grilled bread on the bottom of each soup bowl and ladle the hot soup over, making sure that everyone gets some mussels, prawns (shrimp) and calamari (squid). Add a spoonful of rouille if desired.

- To make the rouille, roast and then skin the bell peppers (capsicums) under a hot grill. Then place bell peppers (capsicums), breadcrumbs, garlic, vinegar, soup liquid and chillies in a food processor and process. Be careful not to over-process. When the ingredients are well mixed add enough olive oil and salt and pepper to make a flavorsome paste.

Salmon Quiche

PASTRY

Serves 4 -6

60g (2 oz) white flour, sifted
60g (2 oz) wholemeal flour
½ teaspoon salt
90g (3 oz) butter
1 egg yolk
1 tablespoon lemon juice

FILLING

4 slices bacon, rind removed and diced
250g (8 oz) tin salmon in brine
3 eggs
100g spinach
375ml (12½fl oz) fresh cream
1 tablespoon parsley, chopped
1 tablespoon Parmesan cheese, grated
½ teaspoon paprika
1 teaspoon salt
freshly ground black pepper, to taste

- Preheat oven to 200°C (400°F).

- To make pastry, mix flours and salt together in a bowl. Rub in the butter with your fingertips, until the mixture resembles fine breadcrumbs. Add egg yolk and lemon juice and mix to form a firm dough (if necessary, add a tablespoon of water). Press the pastry into a 25 cm (10 in) flan tin.

- To make filling, gently fry bacon in a small frying pan. Drain on absorbent paper. Drain and flake salmon, reserving liquid.

- Arrange the salmon on the base of the pastry, then sprinkle bacon on top. In a bowl, beat together reserved salmon liquid, eggs, spinach, cream, parsley, cheese, paprika, salt and pepper.

- Pour mixture gently, over the back of a spoon, into the flan tin to cover salmon and bacon.

- Bake in the oven for 10 minutes then reduce heat to 165°C (325°F) and cook a further 30–35 minutes, or until the filling is set.

Salmon Spread

Serves 4-6

10-15 slices smoked salmon
2 tablespoons dill, freshly chopped
freshly ground black pepper

SALMON SAUCE

3 tablespoons sweet mustard
1 tablespoon French mustard
1 egg yolk
2 tablespoons sugar
2 tablespoons white wine vinegar
200ml (7fl oz) olive oil

- To make the sauce mix all sauce ingredients thoroughly.

- Cut the salmon into thin shreds and bind it with the sauce.

- Season with freshly ground pepper. Serve with crackers or chunky slices of bread and garnish with flat-leaf parsley, chopped chives or fresh dill.

Smoked Oyster Dip

Servse 4

125g (4 oz) cream cheese
1 shallot (scallion),
cut into 25mm (1in) lengths
1 teaspoon lemon juice
100g (3½ oz) canned smoked oysters
salt and freshly ground black pepper
1 packet crackers

- In a food processor, place cream cheese, shallot and lemon juice and beat until smooth, with shallot finely chopped.

- Add smoked oysters with oil, directly from the can with salt and pepper. Pulse in 2 second bursts until oysters are roughly chopped.

- Place in serving bowl, cover and refrigerate. Serve with a selection of crackers.

Baked Fish

Serves 4-6

1 large firm fish cleaned
1 teaspoon salt
¼ teaspoon white pepper
2 onions, sliced
4 ripe tomatoes, skinned and thickly sliced
½ teaspoon ground allspice
¼ teaspoon extra salt
¼ teaspoon black peppercorns, crushed
½ teaspoon cayenne pepper
2 tablespoons brown sugar
125ml (4 fl oz) vinegar
60ml (2fl oz) water
60g (2 oz) butter
Lemon Slices

- Preheat oven to 150°C (300°F).
- Place fish in a greased baking dish and season with salt and pepper. Cover with onion and tomato.
- Sprinkle with allspice, extra salt, peppercorns, cayenne pepper and brown sugar. Add vinegar and water and dot with small pieces of butter.
- Wrap in foil. Bake fish in the oven for 20-30 minutes, depending on the size of fish. Baste frequently.

Poached Fish In White Wine Sauce

Serves 2- 4

750g –1 kg (1½–2lb) fish fillets
375ml (12½fl oz) court bouillon
375ml (12½fl oz) dry white wine
pinch of tarragon
1 small onion, finely chopped
3 egg yolks
3 tablespoons fresh cream
salt and pepper, to taste

- Prepare fish and poach in court bouillon.

- Drain well and keep hot.

- Place wine, tarragon and onion in a saucepan and bring to the boil.

- Add court bouillon and boil continuously, until volume is reduced by half. Allow to cool.

- In a bowl, beat egg yolks with cream. Add to cooled liquid and reheat gently, without boiling.

- Season with salt and pepper, pour over the poached fish fillets, and serve.

Tuna Mornay

Serves 4

500g (1lb) potatoes, boiled
30g (1 oz) margarine
2 tablespoons milk
salt and pepper, to taste
300g (10½ oz) can tuna in brine
315ml (10½fl oz) béchamel sauce
30-60g (2-3 oz) tasty cheese, grated

- Preheat oven to 180°C (350°F).

- Mash the potatoes and beat in the margarine, milk and salt and pepper.

- Line the sides and bottom of a shallow ovenproof dish with mashed potato, then put flaked tuna on top of potato on the bottom of the dish.

- Make (or heat, if it's already made) béchamel sauce, stir in cheese, then spoon sauce over tuna.

- Bake in a moderate oven for 15 minutes or until fish is golden on top.

Béchamel Sauce

315ml (10½ fl oz) milk
1 onion, quartered
1 stalk celery, chopped
1 carrot, chopped
6 black peppercorns
1 blade of mace
1 bay leaf
2 cloves
30g (1 oz) butter
2 tablespoons plain (all-purpose) flour
salt and freshly ground black pepper, to taste

- Place milk, onion, celery, carrot, peppercorns, mace, bay leaf and cloves in the top of a double boiler over gently boiling water.

- Cover the pan and heat very slowly for 30 minutes. Strain and set milk aside.

- Melt butter in a heavy saucepan, stir in flour and cook for 1 minute over a medium heat. Add milk and heat, stirring constantly until boiling. Reduce heat to low and cook for 2 minutes.

- Season with salt and pepper

Index

First published in 2023 by New Holland Publishers,
Sydney Level 1, 178 Fox Valley Road, Wahroonga, 2076,
NSW, Australia

newhollandpublishers.com

Copyright © 2023 New Holland Publishers
Copyright © 2023 in text: New Holland
Copyright © in images: Various sources including
Shutterstock

A record of this book is held at the National Library of
Australia

ISBN : 9781760795481

Group Managing Director: Fiona Schultz
Designer: Ben Taylor (Taylor Design)
Production Director: Arlene Gippert
Printed in China

10 9 8 7 6 5 4 3 2 1

Keep up with New Holland Publishers

f NewHollandPublishers

 @newhollandpublishers